This Doodle By Number
Belongs To

....

By Doodle Lovely

Dessert is like a feel-good song and the best ones make you dance!

CHEF EDWARD LEE

Made in Canada. First printing 2022.
www.DoodleLovely.com

LIFE'S SWEET!

What a delightful treat to play in the kitchen, make a mess and not have to clean up! Roll up your sleeves and try some sweet doodling.

Doodle By Number™ isn't just for kids, it's for anyone who wants to quiet their busy thoughts, awaken their creative spirit, and enjoy the peace that comes with a little mindfulness. And what better treat than to take a bite-size mindful break.

I love sweet treats almost as much as I love doodling, which is why this book is special to me; two feel good activities in one!

You don't need to be an artist or an expert to enjoy doodling. Just like you don't need to be a chef to make delicious treats. You just need a pinch of creativity, a dash of mindfulness and a moment to start.

Enjoy making your life even sweeter!

Melissa x

WHY DOODLE?

It's true that people have been doodling for millennia! "Spontaneous drawing" has been studied and verified as a means to decrease stress in our lives.

Taking pen in hand and using the rhythmic motions of doodling, activates the relaxation response within the brain. Just the thing to calm the chaos and invite more joyful living!

Happiness Boost
Happiness is the result of playfulness. Playfulness in life, including work, increases satisfaction & purpose.

Unleash Creativity
Doodling is known to be the most accessible way of helping the mind relax, so it can spark fresh ideas and creativity.

Encourage Innovation
Doodling helps unlock seemingly unconnected ideas, bringing them together for innovation and problem solving.

DISCOVER THE BENEFITS OF DOODLING TODAY

Greater Productivity
Doodling stimulates new ideas and allows for focus. Even when you're feeling overwhelmed, just five minutes of doodling will help you to refresh, recharge and reset your thoughts.

Increase Your Focus
Doodling promotes your wellbeing by calming your brain and lowering anxiety. It also improves concentration and helps you focus.

Manage Emotions
Doodling is a safe method for processing emotions, converting negative feelings into neutral balance, without judgment.

How to use your

DOODLE *by* NUMBER™

Pick up a pen, your favorite marker, or pencil of any color.

At the bottom of each example page there is a selection of four doodle patterns to choose from. Each pattern is circled and numbered.

Follow the numbers to create a doodle pattern on the opposite page. If you want to use more or less doodles, go for it!

Complete the *Doodle By Number™* and touch it up to your satisfaction.

Feel free to make the doodle your own using your favorite shapes, lines and patterns too. Even add color if you like. Doodle-riffic!

Follow the numbers to match your doodles on the opposite page.

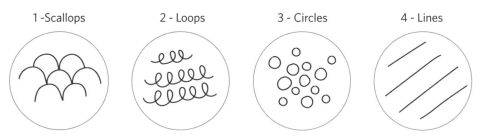

1 - Scallops   2 - Loops   3 - Circles   4 - Lines

A recipe has no soul.
You, as the cook,
must bring soul
to a recipe.

THOMAS KELLER

Follow the numbers to match your doodles on the opposite page.

1 - Drops   2 - Swirls   3 - Circles   4 - Lines

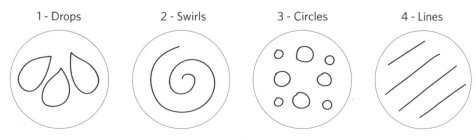

Baking is done out
of love, to share
with family and
friends, to see
them smile.

ANNA OLSON

Follow the numbers to match your doodles on the opposite page.

1 - Short Lines   2 - Stars   3 - Wavy Lines   4 - Peaks

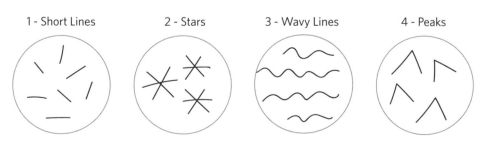

Life is short, make it sweet!

UNKNOWN

Follow the numbers to match your doodles on the opposite page.

1 - Double Scallops

2 - Dots & Stars

3 - Wavy Lines

4 - Lines

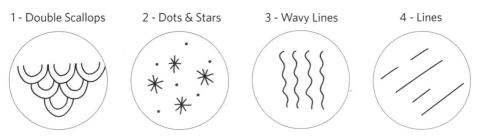

Why not question what can or can't be a layer in layer cake?

CHRISTINA TOSI

Follow the numbers to match your doodles on the opposite page.

1 - Tents   2 - Flowers & Dots   3 - Circles   4 - Scallops

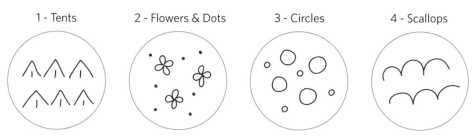

The desire to create is one of the deepest yearnings of the human soul.

DIETER F. UCHTDORF

Follow the numbers to match your doodles on the opposite page.

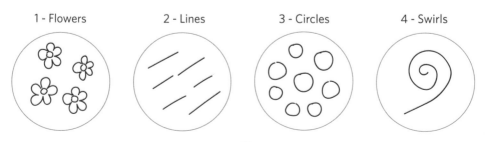

1 - Flowers 2 - Lines 3 - Circles 4 - Swirls

When life is sweet, say thank you and celebrate. And when life is bitter, say thank you and grow.

SHAUNA NIEQUIST

Follow the numbers to match your doodles on the opposite page.

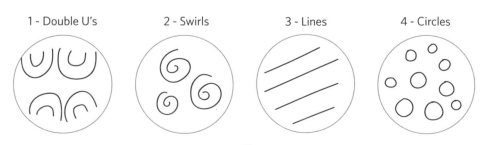

1 - Double U's   2 - Swirls   3 - Lines   4 - Circles

You can't make
everyone happy.
You're not
ice cream.

UNKNOWN

Follow the numbers to match your doodles on the opposite page.

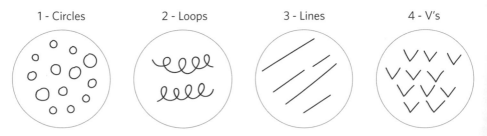

1 - Circles 2 - Loops 3 - Lines 4 - V's

It is the sweet simple things of life which are the real ones after all.

LAURA INGALLS WILDER

Follow the numbers to match your doodles on the opposite page.

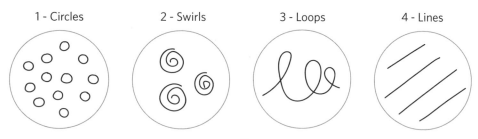

1 - Circles 2 - Swirls 3 - Loops 4 - Lines

*Life is uncertain.
Eat dessert first.*

ERNESTINE ULMER

Follow the numbers to match your doodles on the opposite page.

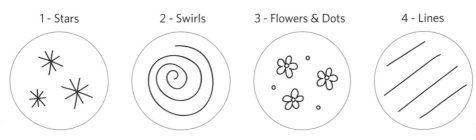

1 - Stars   2 - Swirls   3 - Flowers & Dots   4 - Lines

The secret
ingredient is
always love.

UNKNOWN

Follow the numbers to match your doodles on the opposite page.

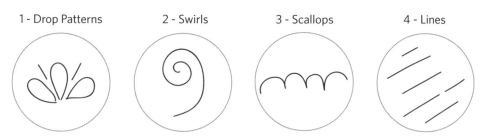

1 - Drop Patterns   2 - Swirls   3 - Scallops   4 - Lines

Never, ever underestimate the importance of having fun.

RANDY PAUSCH

Follow the numbers to match your doodles on the opposite page.

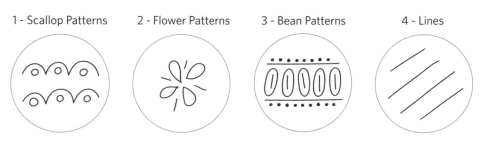

1 - Scallop Patterns   2 - Flower Patterns   3 - Bean Patterns   4 - Lines

I have a sweet tooth. I love dessert, and if somebody makes me one, I'm going to have it.

SARAH RAFFERTY

Follow the numbers to match your doodles on the opposite page.

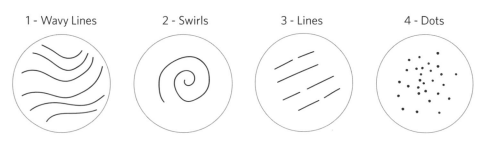

1 - Wavy Lines   2 - Swirls   3 - Lines   4 - Dots

We must have pie.
Stress cannot exist in
the presence of a pie.

DAVID MAMET

Follow the numbers to match your doodles on the opposite page.

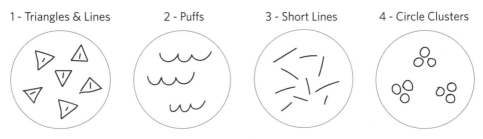

1 - Triangles & Lines

2 - Puffs

3 - Short Lines

4 - Circle Clusters

Donut ever give up.

UNKNOWN

Follow the numbers to match your doodles on the opposite page.

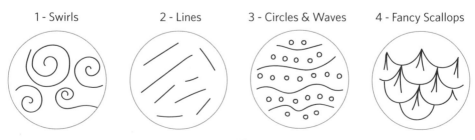

1 - Swirls   2 - Lines   3 - Circles & Waves   4 - Fancy Scallops

Every moment is a fresh beginning.

T.S. ELIOT

Follow the numbers to match your doodles on the opposite page.

1 - Drops   2 - Swirls   3 - Dot Clusters   4 - Lines

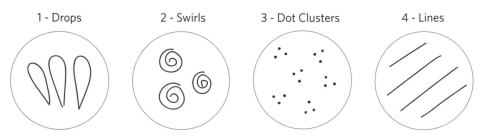

Cupcakes are
muffins
that believed in
miracles.

UNKNOWN

Follow the numbers to match your doodles on the opposite page.

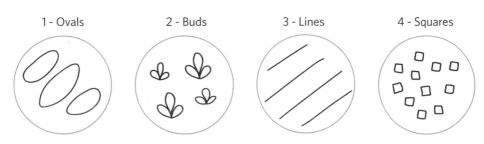

1 - Ovals 2 - Buds 3 - Lines 4 - Squares

Cooking and baking
is both physical and
mental therapy.

MERRY BERRY

Follow the numbers to match your doodles on the opposite page.

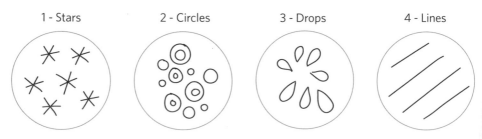

1 - Stars   2 - Circles   3 - Drops   4 - Lines

Follow the numbers to match your doodles on the opposite page.

1 - Circles   2 - Flower Patterns   3 - Rainbows   4 - Lines

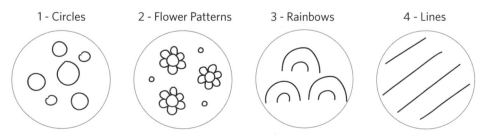

I like to party. And by party I mean stay at home and bake.

UNKNOWN

Follow the numbers to match your doodles on the opposite page.

1 - 'S' Curves   2 - Circles   3 - Stars   4 - Hatching

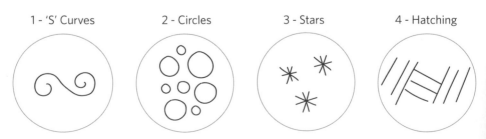

I want to have a good body, but not as much as I want dessert.

JASON LOVE

Follow the numbers to match your doodles on the opposite page.

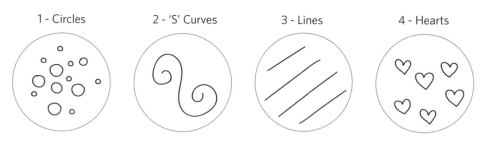

1 - Circles　　2 - 'S' Curves　　3 - Lines　　4 - Hearts

Life is meant
to be lived as a
celebration.

TOPAZ

Follow the numbers to match your doodles on the opposite page.

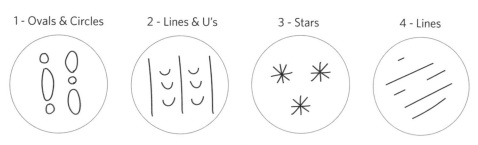

1 - Ovals & Circles   2 - Lines & U's   3 - Stars   4 - Lines

The past is gone. Today is full of possibilities.

KAREN CASEY

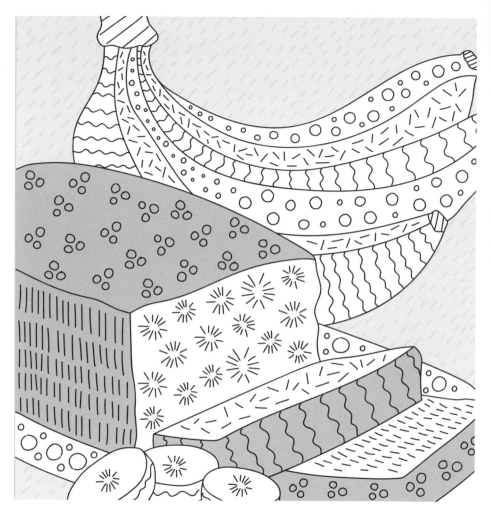

Follow the numbers to match your doodles on the opposite page.

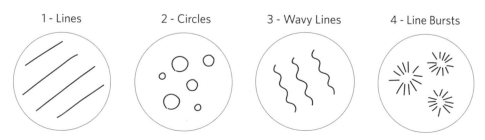

1 - Lines   2 - Circles   3 - Wavy Lines   4 - Line Bursts

When you see a beautiful loaf of bread, slow down, appreciate it, enjoy it, then give yourself a chance to think!

CHRIS GEIGER

Follow the numbers to match your doodles on the opposite page.

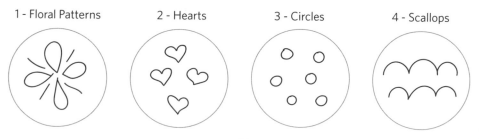

1 - Floral Patterns   2 - Hearts   3 - Circles   4 - Scallops

Cookies are made of
butter and love.

NORWEGIAN PROVERB

Follow the numbers to match your doodles on the opposite page.

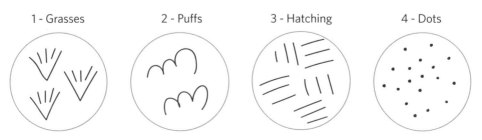

1 - Grasses   2 - Puffs   3 - Hatching   4 - Dots

I just want more hours in a day and cake. That's all.

UNKNOWN

Follow the numbers to match your doodles on the opposite page.

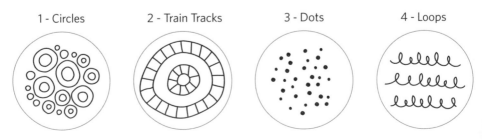

1 - Circles

2 - Train Tracks

3 - Dots

4 - Loops

All dreams are within reach you just have to keep moving towards them.

VIOLA DAVIS

Follow the numbers to match your doodles on the opposite page.

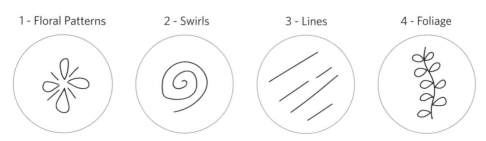

1 - Floral Patterns   2 - Swirls   3 - Lines   4 - Foliage

Life is what you bake it.

UNKNOWN

Follow the numbers to match your doodles on the opposite page.

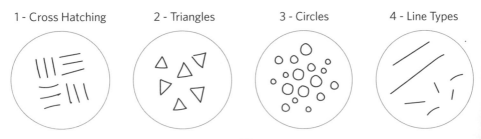

1 - Cross Hatching 2 - Triangles 3 - Circles 4 - Line Types

All you need is love. But a little chocolate now and then doesn't hurt.

CHARLES M. SCHULZ

Follow the numbers to match your doodles on the opposite page.

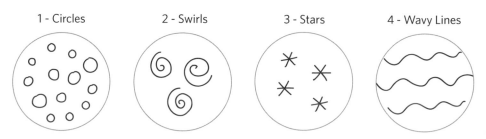

1 - Circles   2 - Swirls   3 - Stars   4 - Wavy Lines

Love at first bite.

UNKNOWN

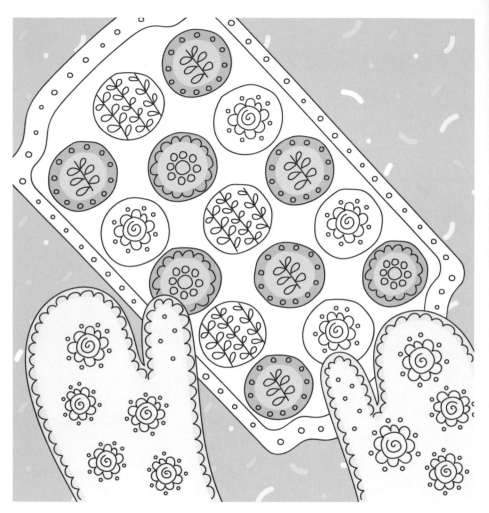

Follow the numbers to match your doodles on the opposite page.

1 - Floral Patterns   2 - Vines   3 - Circles   4 - Scallops

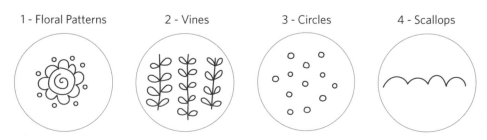

Life is short.
Surround yourself
with good people
and only eat
good cookies.

UNKNOWN

Meet the Doodler

MELISSA LLOYD is an international doodler, designer, teacher, author and inspirationalist. Her passion for creativity can be found globally on products, environments and in the hearts of those with whom she has connected.

Melissa combines her twenty plus years of experience in professional design and communication with her passion for humanity, psychology, art therapy and mindfulness; infusing a deep understanding of self.

Melissa teaches soul-care through creative practices and encourages you to learn how to navigate the stormy seas of life, reducing stress and rejuvenating your mind.

By honoring your creative soul and the celebration of living in the moment, Melissa inspires you to bring joy back into your life by finding a place of peace internally. Her transformational approach to creativity, through doodling and living, inspires others to live a healthier and happier life. 'Always Be You... For You.'

Melissa balances her time between mothering, creating, teaching and living in her little Cottage By The Sea. To discover more of Melissa's work visit:
DoodleLovely.com

Be happy for this moment.
This moment is your life.

OMAR KHAYYAM

Did you enjoy this *Doodle By Number*™? We would love to hear your feedback!
Please email us: **hello@doodlelovely.com**

Connect with us to know when the next edition of the *Pocket Doodle By Number*™
will be available at our online shop.
DoodleLovely.com

NEXT TITLES IN THIS
POCKET DOODLE BY NUMBER™ SERIES

Intermediate

Expert